Dear Apple in progress,

Thank you for taking the challenge of reading this book. We designed it with you in mind. Understanding that your time is valuable, we built this book on the idea that one phrase a week will move you on your journey to become an Apple. An Apple is an individual who is recognized as valuable and has the ability to impact others in a positive way. They are the Apple of someone's eye. They Shine!

You can read this book anyway you choose. You will read 52 " Impact Phrases and Questions." Each is accompanied by a small paragraph to enhance your reading. At the end, you will find thought stimulating questions, statements and suggestions. We call them "WHATCHA GONNA DO ABOUT IT?" moments. We suggest you take time to really reflect and answer the questions during the year. Take some additional time to review your answers in order to discover how things have changed.

This book is one way for us to stay connected with you. As you are progressing through this book or when you are done, email us and let us know how this book impacted your life. Our goal is that you are not just living a life, but living a dynamic life. A Life of Growth and Achievement.

It is time to get started and it all begins with one simple question...

"Are you ready to Shine?"

Happy Reading,

Frank and Rodger

Are you an APPLE?

-1-

"Are you an Apple?"

An Apple is someone who is building and developing an attitude which produces powerful Leaders, Lovers and Leaners. Apples are dynamic individuals who others seek to be around because of their character and accomplishments. Apples not only increase their value through achievement but also by motivating and inspiring others to achieve as well. Daily, Apples put forth the proper attitude and effort to achieve their purpose. Apples are highly motivated for Success. They Shine and they Shine Bright! Now that you know what an Apple is, it's time to get your shine on!

Whatcha gonna do about it?

What makes you an APPLE and why?

Who do you identify as a Quality APPLE?

What qualities do they possess that you admire?

Take some time this week and identify the quality Apples in your life. Be sure to connect with them this week to let them know you appreciate them and why.

What attitudes do you need to improve in order to achieve more?

How you will address these attitudes during this week.

BELIEF

- 2 -

Do you have Belief, Action, and Determination?

Belief, Action and Determination are necessary to achieve your dreams. You must have a dream to believe in. You must take the proper actions to make your dream come true. When tough times occur (and they will) you must stay determined. Your Determination will give you the energy to continue your actions. Your actions will re-establish your belief. Without Belief, Action and Determination achievement dies before it begins. Apples make dreams a reality. Apples Believe, Act and Stay Determined.

Whatcha gonna do about it?

What Dreams do you have right now?

What dreams of yours have faded over time?

Why do you believe they faded over time?

Is there a Dream which needs to come back into focus? What actions you can take this week to re energize that Dream?

- 3 -

"Are you Valuable?"

Yes you are!! You are an Apple! You have Value! You have Impact! You have the ability to impact the lives of people (including yourself) in a positive way. When you do this you show your true value. Treat people like they are valuable. Treat people like they will impact your life in a positive way. Value knows Value. It's amazing what is possible when you choose to see people as Apples. Value is more than a price tag. Be the Apple for someone today!

Whatcha gonna do about it?

Who are the positive people in your life?

In what ways do you value your relationship with them?

How can you make a positive impact on 3 of those relationships this week?

"Take a moment to make that Impact and show your Value."

- 4 -
"What's underneath your skin?"

The apple is covered by a colorful, protective skin. It provides a protective shield from weather, pests, and other environmental disturbances. However, the true value of an apple is what lies beneath the skin, the flesh. Like apples, we put up protective shields of attitudes and behaviors which protect us from negative people, challenging situations, and other environmental disturbances. However, our real value comes from the substance of who we really are. What's underneath your skin?

Whatcha gonna do about it?

In what ways do you put up a protective shield?

Why do you feel the need to have those protective shields?

What actions can you take this week to let others get to know you better?

In what ways are you taking care of the internal you...your emotional and your spiritual sides?

"If you are having trouble taking care of the internal you, find someone to help you work through this matter."

- 5 -

"You reap what you sow, so plant wisely!"

Apple seeds contain critical information for the development of new plants and new growth. Planted in a rich environment, the seeds can produce new orchards. Within you lies the seeds of achievement. Once planted in a rich and supportive environment, growth and achievement will flourish. A new orchard of ideas, possibilities and leaders are the result of dedicated seed care. Apple seeds yield sweet fruit desired by all, so plant wisely!

Whatcha gonna do about it?

What is something you wish to accomplish?

What seeds do you need to plant?

Do you have a rich environment in your life where you can plant your seeds of achievement?

What actions can you take this week to enrich the environment around you?

- 6 -

Are you willing to put in the Big Work?

You have dreams. Some big, Some small. They need the proper nourishment, time and energy to grow. You are an apple. The world is full of apples. Some apples are a little bigger and some are a little smaller. No matter the size of the apple, the same process is required to make them grow...The achievement of dreams. Nothing is wrong with having a big dream or a small dream. The important thing is to turn your dreams into reality. Set the bar high and put in the necessary work to make your dreams come true. When you do, you grow as an Apple! Go Big. Work Big. Live Big!

Whatcha gonna do about it?

Do you only "talk" about your dreams or do you take the necessary actions to make them a reality? Why?

Does having a big dream scare you? Why?

This week, set one big dream you feel you can live this year.

- 7 -

"Are you Strong to the Core?"

The most vital part of the apple is the Core. Strength, support and seeds reside within the core. Without a solid core, there is no fruit. As an apple, your core is what propels your growth. The core is where the values and convictions you possess collide with your passion and desire. This dynamic concoction provides the energy for you to grow every day. If your core is not strong, there is no achievement. A rotted core yields stunted fruit. Your core matters!

Whatcha gonna do about it?

Have you taken a look at your values and belief system lately?

In what ways are they in need of enhancing?

Do your values conflict with the dreams you have?

How have you altered your dreams to match your values?

16

- 8 -

"I may not be the smartest person in the world, but I do have eyes!"

A book can teach you about a subject, but your eyes show you the truth. You don't have to have a wall full of degrees to prove that you're smart. Intelligence can come from practical experience and observation. You can learn a lot by reading, but you learn so much more by actually experiencing what you read about. Books give knowledge, but Experience is the teacher.

Whatcha gonna do about it?

Who are the people you consider intelligent? Why?

How did they gain their knowledge?

How have you gained your intelligence?

In what 3 ways can you use your intelligence (experience) this week?

18

- 9 -

"You can't go somewhere physically until you go there mentally"

Every great accomplishment in history came from a vision. Before you can do something physically, you must visualize it in your mind. The vision becomes an idea. The idea becomes a thought. The thought gets played over and over again in your head until you do it. It is amazing when you experience an idea go from thought...to paper...to reality. When you mentally commit to an idea, the chances of the idea becoming a physical reality are amplified. Remember, if you think rotten things, rotten things will happen! Get positive by thinking positive.

Whatcha gonna do about it?

Are you mentally prepared for the week ahead?

How do you mentally prepare yourself for the week ahead?

What is your biggest challenge to staying positive?

What is your vision for the week?

"Write the vision down and read that vision daily when you wake up and before you go to bed."

- 10 -

"Are you living on purpose or just going through the motions?"

      When playing sports, a player must move according to how the play was designed and with purpose. The athlete must play within his or her strengths and with the proper behavior or they will be removed from competition. Life is a competition. It is a battle for your mind, your energy and your time. When you move with purpose and control, your actions set the stage for daily achievement and growth. Purpose is the winning play for the game called Life!

Whatcha gonna do about it?

Do you have a current purpose (a reason to dream)?
What is it?

What are your strengths ?   Write them down here

How are your strengths moving you toward your
purpose?

*"We all have a purpose. If you are unsure of your
purpose, Find someone who can assist you in
clarifying your purpose."*

-11 -

"Is Your life a P.A.R.T.Y.?"

Everyone enjoys a great party. Lots of food, fun and connecting. Once someone gains the reputation of throwing great parties, everyone looks forward to the invite. Your Life is a **P.A.R.T.Y**! It has a **Purpose**, focused on **Achievement**, built on **Relationships** and grown over **Time**. Of course, the end result is **You**. To enjoy the PARTY life, you have to invite the right party goers to join you in the celebration. Remember, there's more fun when there is more than one. You bring the PARTY with you! Make it a great one.

Whatcha gonna do about it?

Every party needs the right guests. Who's on your VIP list of party goers for your Life PARTY?

Why are these individuals on your VIP list?

What kind of PARTY do you want your life to reflect?

What kind of guests do you let into your PARTY?

Are there some guests that need to be removed from the VIP list?

ACTION

- *12* -

"Have you picked your fruit?"

Your dreams are like fruit! Dreams don't just happen, you have to make them happen. You have to pick the ones you really want. You can't just wait for the fruit to fall out of a tree, because you never know what you'll get. You could get something good, something rotten or something that isn't ready. You have to go pick your fruit. Don't let the fruit pick you. The more fruit you pick ,the more options and choices you will have.

Whatcha gonna do about it?

Have you identified a dream that is ready to come true? Write it here.

With whom can you share this dream ?

 Make time this week to share your dream with someone.

- 13 -

"Are you willing to take a Bite out of life?"

In order to enjoy all life has to offer, you must take a bite. The greatest challenge to growth is the willingness to step out into the unknown. You must be willing to try something new. When you try something new, you grow! In order for you to have the full experience of life, you need to challenge yourself beyond what you know. You must embrace the unknown as a welcome partner on your journey. You must be willing to take a Bite out of life!

Whatcha gonna do about it?

**The first bite is always the hardest. (What bite do you need to take to grow
this week?)**

What other bites do you need to take?

What are three positive things that will result after you take a bite this week?

- 14 -

"Dream Big, Dream Often!"

Children are great dreamers. They have the best attitudes about life. They dream of being the biggest, strongest, toughest person ever. They are the best at everything and nothing can stand in their way. They believe in themselves so much that nothing is impossible. When faced with a setback, they call "Do Over" in order to get it right. They dream day in and day out. Successful individuals have this "childlike " attitude to life. They believe with the proper information, they can be the best. They believe they can achieve anything with the right connections. When successful people face life's challenges, they see them as "Do Overs" to learn from. The successful never stop dreaming. They Dream Big and Dream Often.

Whatcha gonna do about it?

Do you wish you could have a "Do Over?"

What is one "Do Over" you would like?

What can you learn from this "Do Over?"

- 15 -

"Are you living inspired or just living tired?"

Dreams give us excitement, creative release and unimaginable hope. Dreams inspire us. Yet, evening dreams fade quickly when faced with the reality of the day. You have a purpose in life. The difficulty is pursuing it. A purposeful dream becomes a nightmare when not pursued. This leaves you suffering from restlessness,weariness and bitterness. Successful individuals know the value of living their dreams. They dream both day and night. Are you living your dreams?

Whatcha gonna do about it?

What are the most inspiring places in your life?

What makes this place inspiring to you?

After visiting that inspiring place, what are you inspired to do this week? Do it!

"If you can travel to this inspirational place, visit it this week. If not, How can you create that same inspired feeling where you are right now?"

- 16 -

"Victory tastes sweet because preparation takes time."

Preparation is the first step to achieving. The farmer can't embark without a plan. She can't engage without the right tools. She can't excel without the right elements in place. She may have soil, but if she does not plow, it will not be ready to receive the seed. If she does not spread the fertilizer, the seed may not grow. If she does not protect the seedlings, the crop will die. If she does not have a storage barn, she cannot receive the harvest. Preparation does not come without effort. It does not come in an instant. Preparation takes time. The farmer can only enjoy the sweetness of her labor once the environment for the fruit to grow has been prepared. Excellence comes only when we struggle to make things happen. Without preparation there is no success. Success is the sweet fruit of victory over struggle. Make time to prepare for the sweet enjoyment of your success.

Whatcha gonna do about it?

What causes delays in your preparation process?

How can you address these challenges?

How do you prepare to achieve your dreams?

How will you prepare this week?

- 17 -

"Are you willing to do the Sugar Honey Ice Tea jobs?"

No one ever wants to do the **S**-ugar **H**-oney **I**-ce **T**-ea jobs. Sadly, these are an important part of life. With every dream, there is a dirty job that must be completed to achieve that dream. Many times you want to delegate or assign these crappy jobs to other people. If your dream is important to you, you must be willing and able to do the "Sugar Honey Ice Tea Jobs." Are you willing to roll your sleeves up and get dirty?

Whatcha gonna do about it?

What are your current feelings on Sugar Honey Ice Tea jobs ?

Do you run from the dirty job that must get done?

What can you do this week to overcome a dirty job?

- 18 -

"Are you Producing or just Occupying?"

The third step in Apple development is production. Without fruit a tree has not reached its potential. Without fruit a tree is not matured. Without quality fruit a tree has not fulfilled its purpose. It is merely taking up space. If you possess great qualities, and knowledge, but don't produce, you have not reached your potential. If you are not leading and teaching others, you are not mature. If you are not producing quality results, you are not fulfilling your purpose, you are merely occupying space.

Whatcha gonna do about it?

Reflect on your life to this point, when have you been most productive?

What are you capable of teaching others?

Who can you share your knowledge and experience with this week?

- 19 -

"Plant some seeds!"

The farmer has a great vision. He sees a field that can be transformed into an orchard of consistently producing fruit trees. However, the vision will never be realized until the farmer plants some seeds. He must gather the proper seeds, prepare the land and place the seeds into rich soil. You too have great visions of success . However, you cannot achieve until you gather the information necessary to achieve your vision. You must prepare your environment to accept the end results. Most of all you must take action and plant some seeds. If you don't seed, you'll only get weeds.

Whatcha gonna do about it?

You have a great vision of success. What does it look like? Write down your vision now.

What seeds of information do you need to gather this week to grow your vision?

List what you need to do this week to prepare the land to receive this seed.

- 20 -

"Are you Bored with Life? Grab a Napkin!"

Napkins are used everyday. They are used to celebrate and commemorate special events. They are used for advertising businesses. They are used for clearing the mind of creative thoughts. Simply put, Napkins are Dream Collectors. It all begins with good friends and food. Discussions start. Discussions about all types of topics, then someone says, "What if!" Like a bolt of lighting, creativity hits the room. The wildest ideas that seem somewhat possible, get placed upon the nearest napkin. Unfortunately, we don't always see the value right away. The napkin gets crumpled into a pocket and then runs through the washer. The dream is gone. Dreams are valuable and impactful. They move us forward and give us hope. They allow our creativity to shine.

When you need a creative moment, step out with some close friends, grab some good food and enjoy a great conversation. The time invested will lift your spirits and get the creative juices flowing again. Grab that napkin and write, but don't waste the dream. Treasure the writing, for it might be the dream that changes the world.

Whatcha gonna do about it?

When lightning strikes this week, do you have the proper device to capture your ideas? What is the device?

Gather with your core friends this week, share with them a bit of information about your dreams and see where the conversation goes.

- 21 -

"Celebrate the milestones, or they will become grindstones!"

The farmer understands that when farming an apple tree, it takes up to four years to see fruit. Yet, the farmer continues to toil and labor day in and day out. Why? Because the farmer knows that a celebration is just around the corner. When the farmer sees the little sprout come out of the ground, there is celebration. Her labor has not been in vain. The labor has produced life and growth. She knows that the tree, when old enough can bear fruit for over 20 years.

Your life is full of little moments of growth. The question is, "Are you cultivating an atmosphere of celebration?" Each step brings you closer to your dream. Each growth brings you closer to your purpose. If you can celebrate the success of others, why can't you celebrate your own successes? Each step is the preparation for your achievements. Each achievement brings you more celebration. The more you celebrate, the less your life seems like a chore.

Whatcha gonna do about it?

Do you celebrate the little things? What do you do to celebrate them?

What milestones do you need to celebrate?

How will you celebrate a recent achievement this week and with whom?

DETERMINATION

-22 -

"Success begins in your head!"

When we review success, four basic elements come through clearly. Success is created by the **Vision** to see what others cannot. Success is initiated by the **Decision** to follow the vision. Success is fueled by a **Passion** and desire to accomplish. Finally, success is achieved through the **Motion** of creating a plan and then acting upon it. When these elements are present, success is sure to follow.

Whatcha gonna do about it?

Review your relationships. This week, who can you assist move their vision towards decision?

What steps can you take this week to build a culture of success?

- 23 -

"You just gotta get there!"

Sometimes it doesn't matter how you get there. It just matters that you get there.

In life we often worry about what is going to happen down the road. We worry that we are not achieving in the same manner as others we admire. We worry that things won't go as we planned. We worry when we are asked or forced to step out of our comfort zone. We worry when we seek something that we cannot immediately see. We even worry when we hope and pray for something to happen. Stop worrying! The most important priority is that you get there. Nothing happens if you don't take that first step. Worrying prevents action from occurring. Action must occur in order to live your achievement.

Whatcha gonna do about it?

Looking at your dreams, what are the bear necessities to accomplish them?

What do you worry about that prevents you from accomplishing your dreams?

What steps can you take this week to move one step closer to achieving your dreams?

- 24 -

" If you have to be something, be Something Else!"

In this life you must be something. You will be a parent, a worker, a child, a partner, a friend...Something! You have the choice to go with the crowd, be a number and do what others are doing. Or you can choose to be special...Something Else! You can choose to be better, wiser, stronger...Something Else! Those who have achieved the greatest success, are those who have chosen to be Something Else! They choose to be something of Value and to leave an Impact. So, the question really is, "Are you stirring things up or just going with the flow?

Whatcha gonna do about it?

How can you bring excellence to your roles in life?

What can you do this week to encourage someone to see the positives in life?

This week, don't try to be someone else. Go out and do something to show your uniqueness.

- 25 -

"Life Happens!"

The board game Life taught us many things. It taught us that choices lead us to different paths. It taught us to mind our money. It taught us that the more kids you have, the larger car you need. Most of all it taught us that there are things that are outside our control. In the real game of Life, the same lessons are true. Choices have consequences. Watching your finances are important. The more kids you have the more of everything you need. But most of all, there are a lot of things outside of your control. In order to win at this game, control what you can and recognize that *Life Happens* and adjust accordingly.

Whatcha gonna do about it?

In what way does the game of Life have the upper hand ?

What choices are you struggling with?

What three steps can you take this week to change direction?

54

- 26 -

"Can a Bruised Apple be Saved?"

A bruised apple looks beat up, nasty and gross. The truth is, you can often cut away the damaged skin and find the valuable flesh still intact. Like an Apple, you can get bruised by negative people, the daily grind and self doubt. Your "skin" tells a story. Your facial expressions, body language, attitudes and behaviors may unknowingly send the message that you are beat up, nasty and gross. However, under the skin lies a great person. If you take the time to address and "cut away" your damaged areas, you may find more people interested in what you have to offer. You will discover that a bruised apple can be saved!

Whatcha gonna do about it?

Does your skin reflect the correct image of who you really are?

Have others told you that you possess elements (facial expressions, body language, attitudes, habits, and behaviors) which are bruising to yourself and others? What are they?

What three things can you do this week to "cut away" your bruising elements?

What three things can you do this week to visually show the world who you really are?

- 27 -

"Get sauced on life!"

Applesauce is an awesome, multipurpose substance. It can be used as a side dish for a meal. It can be eaten as a dessert. It can be used as a healthy alternative in baking. It brings joy to those that consume it. Applesauce is created by placing chopped apples, sugar and spices in a contained environment. The application of heat and pressure results in the succulent treat.

Negative life experiences often challenge us and leave us chopped up emotionally. This is when we need to sprinkle in the sugar and spice of quality and diverse relationships. These relationships provide us with hope and inspiration. Life puts us under heat and pressure daily. Through this growth process we gain greater substance. A quality, succulent substance that brings joy to those around us. It's time to get sauced!

Whatcha gonna do about it?

Are you experiencing some heat in your life right now? If yes, what is it?

Describe a "high pressure" experience you have had that helped you grow personally or professionally.

This week, write down ten qualities you possess that make you a "succulent treat."

-28 -

"How's your Pest Control?"

Bugs and pests can wreak havoc on an apple orchard. Some pests discolor the skin of apples. Some bury themselves within the flesh and create a nasty taste. Others burrow themselves into the core and destroy the apple from the inside out. Pest in your life can destroy your ability to be an apple recognized as valuable. Pests such as drama, office politics, distrust, anger and poor communication can lead to devastation. Pests invade your life with stealth and might. They devour focus, destroy your home, and can wreak havoc on your health. Farmers meet pests with a plan of action...Pest Control! In order to have a bright future, remove the pest and expect the best.

Whatcha gonna do about it?

Do you have a plan to minimize the pest in your life? What is it?

In what ways do you create pests for others?   What will you do this week to eliminate these behaviors?

What will you do this week to eliminate the pest from your life?

- 29 -

"The right perspective can weather any storm!"

Just as there are seasons of the year, there are seasons in our life. Seasons when we plant the seeds of our dreams. Seasons when we water and protect our dreams from the scorching heat of criticism and frustration. Seasons to pick the harvest of achievement in life. Season for resting and preparing for our next success. Storm clouds of change will be a constant part of our life. However, with the right perspective, we can weather any storm.

Whatcha gonna do about it?

What do you do when something gets in the way of your dream? Do you give up or readjust?

Are your strategies disruptive to or effective for your growth?

What will you do this week to protect your dreams from an impending storm?

-30 -

"Get rid of your buts!"

We often create difficulties in our lives because we allow the word "But" to get in the way. *"But it won't help." "But it can't stop the pain." "But it never works."* That little word, "But", clouds our vision and de-energizes us. Over time, these "Buts" accumulate, leaving us empty and drained.

The words "What if", allows us think positively again. *"What if it would help?" "What if we can stop the pain?" "What if it always comes true?"* The "Whats" de-cloud the mind and energize us with confidence. At the end of the day, Buts make you nuts, What ifs make you strut.

Whatcha gonna do about it?

When others are sharing their thoughts and ideas, how often do you say "but" as a response?

How often do you use the word "but" in your own thinking?

What will you do this week to change your "Buts" into "What Ifs?"

- 31 -

"Do you D.E.A.L. with roadblocks or create them?"

Life is full of roadblocks that can prevent you from achieving your dreams. Many are self-created. These mental roadblocks can delay you or prevent you from achieving your dreams. In order to achieve, there are three things that you must stop doing: Stop Trying, Stop Caring and Stop Worrying. Stop trying to be someone you're not. Stop caring about the opinions of people who don't care about you. Finally, stop worrying about things you can not control.

You must learn to DEAL! **D**on't **E**ver **A**ccept **L**ess of yourself! When you do this, you work to make yourself better. You only value the opinions of people who care about you. You only think about the things you can control. You maximize your efforts and avoid creating a Life full of roadblocks, traffic jams and detours. You achieve!

Whatcha gonna do about it?

Do you constantly compare yourself with others? Why do you do this?

Do you let people's opinions bring you down? Do these people truly value who you are?

Do you constantly worry about things you can't control?

What are the best things about you?

This week, stop trying, caring and worrying and start living!

BUILDING
&
DEVELOPING

- 32 -

"Building and Developing = Success!"

The more you dream about something, the further away that dream becomes. Success is the achievement of a Dream. Dreams don't just happen, they must be grown. Dreams must be nurtured. A dream that didn't come true becomes a nightmare. You must Build And Develop your dreams. When you Build And Develop your dreams, you are growing. When your dreams become reality, that is success!

Whatcha gonna do about it?

Write down one dream you want to Build And Develop this year?

What do you need to make this dream a reality?

What is your plan to make this dream a reality?

Who can help you?

What will you do this week to start Building And Developing this dream?

- 33 -

"A.S.K. - Always Seek Knowledge!"

You never lose ground asking questions! You either stay in the same place or progress forward with the information gained. Asking questions is the beginning of wisdom. If you don't ask questions of yourself and of others you can not grow. Asking questions causes you to admit that you don't know everything and therefore must seek knowledge. The more we ask, the more knowledge we gain. The more we gain, the more we advance in our growth process. The more we grow, the better our production. Asking questions is powerful because it is the key to unlocking the treasure of possibilities. The greatest form of wealth is knowledge. **Always Seek Knowledge!**

Whatcha gonna do about it?

You have a dream, what questions are you ASKing to help you achieve it?

What are the answers to the three questions?

The three questions you should ask about your dreams this week are: *"What do I want? What is it's value to me? How do I get it?"*

What steps can you take to prepare, plan, and execute the answers to the question above?

- 34 -

"Who are the Apples of your Eyes?"

In the age of social media it is difficult to truly know someone. You may believe you know someone based on the information that they reveal about themselves online. However, you cannot truly know them until you take the time to understand them. Make time to build and develop relationships with individuals who can make you better. Make time to know people who are successful in building and developing their dreams. When you make time to investigate and foster supportive relationships now, your investment will yield successful results in the future.

Whatcha gonna do about it?

Who are the New Apples of your eyes (Individuals who are building and developing their dreams) that you need to know?

How will you invest in other Apples this week?

How can you create consistent quality time with individuals who you can support?

- 35 -

"Learning is Living!"

Learning is living and living is learning. Learning is the process of gathering information, processing the information and applying the information for your growth and development. Learning is a constant process that can not be placed within the confines of four walls. It occurs when you engage your senses. Learning is challenging your mind to receive, review, and retain quality information for later use. This increases your knowledge power, which increases your potential to achieve. The final test of the knowledge is how and when you apply that knowledge. Learning is an ongoing process of seeding, gathering and applying. When you Live your Learn. Stay Living!

Whatcha gonna do about it?

In order to achieve your dream, what do you need to learn?

Where can you go this week to learn a skill or acquire knowledge?

How will this knowledge help you build and develop your dream?

- 36 -

"Field Trips Help you Grow!"

Growth occurs when you step out of your comfort zone. This can happen mentally or physically. You need to take field trips. You must travel to the places where you can Ask questions, connect with other dreamers, and constantly be learning mindset. You must go to the places that will help you build and develop your Dreams. It's time to get uncomfortable and take a road trip!

Whatcha gonna do about it?

What places can you go this week to Build and Develop your dreams?

What value do these places hold?

What impact will they have on you building and developing your dreams?

Write down a time where you stepped out of your comfort zone and grew personally or professionally from the experience?

What did you learn from that experience?

- 37 -

"Live it!"

Building and Developing = Success. When you "Live it" you are doing successful things. You are not just doing things for yourself, but you are also helping others experience success. You are being a mentor and a role model. Living your dreams is an amazing feeling. Helping someone else achieve their dreams is magic! To "Live it" means you are building and developing your skills, your relationships and your community. So, Live it and Live it Proud!

Whatcha gonna do about it?

What "Live it" activities can you do for yourself this week?

Who can you teach or mentor to "Live it" this week?

What can you learn by helping someone else "Live it?"

- 38 -

"Plant yourself in a Rich Environment!"

Every apple farmer knows that the process of taking their apple farm from vision to reality takes time and effort. She must be conscious of her environment. She knows that no amount of toil and labor will make plants grow, unless the environment is rich and conditioned. She has two choices: condition the environment with additional products or find a new environment. In our lives, we find ourselves in environments which we know are not conducive to our growth. Two choices exist: help change the environment for the better or find a new environment. Make your environment Rich and Dine on the Sweet Fruit it produces.

Whatcha gonna do about it?

What are the ideal conditions for you to function at your best?

What can you do to create these conditions?

What can you do this week to create an environment for you to produce a healthy mental, physical and spiritual environment for yourself?

- 39 -

"Are you in Rich Environment or Poor Environment?"

To plant yourself in a rich environment, you must understand the difference between Rich Environments and Poor Environments. Rich Environments are supportive places for you to live, work or play in. They are personally and professionally nourishing. Poor Environments are identified by the negative effects people, places and things have on your attitude and health. Real success gets its roots from rich environments. Identify the right environment for your success and get planted quickly.

Whatcha gonna do about it?

Describe the best environment you have ever worked in or experienced?

What made it a Rich Environment?

Are you currently planted in a Rich Environment?

What can you do this week to plant yourself in a Rich Environment?

- 40 -

"Desire success, not just stuff!"

Apples are focused on growth and development. They believe success is a process not a destination. They seek greater involvement, greater connection and greater knowledge. They are never satisfied until they are gaining and attaining. The more Apples grow, the more respect they gain, the more responsibility they achieve and stronger their relationships become. With these gains apples attain greater experiences and influence in life. This process of Gaining and Attaining yields more achievement. It's how Apples experience success.

Whatcha gonna do about it?

What do you desire?

Do you desire things over experiences or interactions with people?

How will these desires help you achieve?

In what ways are you gaining and attaining?

- 41 -

"Share your vision,
Live your dreams!"

A farmer with a great vision shares it with those that can help make it come true. Some may doubt, some may question, but those that understand the vision stick around to help. The farmer lives his farming dream with the support of those who care. If you have a dream and don't share it, you deny someone the opportunity to help you live your dream. No matter how big or small your dream, if you don't share it, you decrease your chances of living it.

Whatcha gonna do about it?

In what ways do you communicate your vision?

Who can assist you with the vision? Make it a point to connect with them this week.

What does your life look like when you're living your dream?

- 42 -

"Apples Shine!"

This is the age of constant self reflection. "Does this make me look fat?" "Does this make my butt look big?" These questions seek to find out if you live up to the norm. It also hints at a sense of doubt. The real question is, "Does this reveal the image that you want to project?"

Your clothing, your mannerisms, your actions, and your thoughts are utilized to communicate a message. A message you hope others will recognize with the same passion you put into it. Instead of asking whether you "live up to the norm," you need to set your own norm and answer the question, "Does this make my Apple Shine?" The bigger your confidence, the better everything looks on you, in you, and through you. The apples with the biggest shine standout and get chosen.

Whatcha gonna do about it?

What image do you project? How do people receive it?

What is the image you want to project ?

Do you show your confidence? Is yes, How? If no, why not?

- 43 -

"Your Success is sys-STEM-ic!"

Are you habitually growing or perpetually slowing? When we review the processes of successful individuals, two things are very apparent. One, their success is affected by the connections they make. Two, their success is a process based on habits which produce a desired result. Just as the apple uses the stem for growth when connected to the tree, growth happens when you connect yourself with individuals who challenge and nourish you. The apple stem carries nutrients and information for reproduction to the core of the apple in order for it to grow and be replicated. As Apples, we must have a system of transferring the knowledge gained into repeated action. Achievement of a dream is not sporadic when it is sySTEMic.

Whatcha gonna do about it?

Who are the five people you spend the most time with?

Do these people inspire you to grow?

Do you know any individuals or groups that will help you grow both personally and professionally?

Do you know how to connect with them?

Who can you do this week to start the process?

- 44 -

"A Hook Up is just a Hook Up, but a Connection lasts forever!"

Relationships are started in a moment. Whether or not they last depends on the parties involved. Some relationships are like a tow truck and a car...they hook up for a short while. Others are like locomotives and train cars...they are connected for a long journey. Every relationship has its benefits. Only a few have long lasting value. Your life is a journey. Are you looking for long-term benefits or a short term fix?

Whatcha gonna do about it?

Do you value connections?

How do you connect and develop relationships?

Is the process effective or can you improve upon it?

Have you taken the time to reflect and understand what makes a great connection?

What are the elements of a great relationship you currently possess?

Use the information gained to strengthen all of your relationships.

This week, sit down with someone you've been connected with for a long period of time and ask them, "What makes our relationship work?"

- 45 -

"S.E.X.Y. is more than skin deep."

Lets face it, being sexy sells. SEXY is attractive, alluring and inviting. However, SEXY is more than skin deep. It comes straight from your core. It comes from the **S**trength of your character. It comes from the **E**ngaging nature of your leadership style. It is showcased by the **EX**pression of your thoughts and ideas through your communication. This all creates who **Y**ou become. SEXY isn't just physical, it's the attitude of confidence. It is the belief you have in yourself that creates a SEXY You.

Whatcha gonna do about it?

What do you do to show your SEXY side?

What abilities or traits do you possess that give you great confidence about yourself?

- 46 -

"Leadership S.U.C.K.S.!"

Leaders have the ability to inspire and motivate
an individual or groups to accomplish a dream or a goal.
Leadership involves taking steps others would not. It
requires handling situations others dare not. It also
means taking bruises that others could not. Leadership
SUCKS! Leadership **S**trongly **U**tilizes **C**ircumstances to
Kick **O**ff **S**uccess. Circumstances in your life will build
who you will become in the future. In life you will be
called to lead. You may not be given a title or preferred
parking spot, but there will be times when you must lead
teams, projects, families and most importantly yourself.
You are a leader. When the road gets rocky, leaders
recognize that success is just around the corner. Battle
scars today lead to success stories in the future.

Whatcha gonna do about it?

List three recent challenging circumstances in your life?

How did you overcome these challenging circumstances?

What did you learn from the circumstances that you can use this week to kick out your next success?

- 47 -

"Save the Drama for your Mama!"

Conflict occurs when unfulfilled expectations and intense emotions collide. Sprinkle in a lack of communication and you've got the recipe for Drama. Drama results from not appreciating the necessity of conflict. Without healthy conflict, we lack the opportunity for improvement. Poor management of conflict leads to Drama. Drama is something that is only entertaining when played out on stage or television! It starts with something small and ends up in a pile of broken hearts, battered attitudes and soiled reputations. Loved by some and feared by others, Drama leaves us cold, callous and caustic... and only a mama can love someone like that!

Whatcha gonna do about it?

What communication strategies do you use during a conflict situation? Are they effective?

How can you avoid Drama in your life roles?

Is there a dramatic situation that you have created? What steps can you take this week to resolve this situation?

- 48 -

"Rottenness brings Disaster!"

It is always good to be Building and Developing. This means that you are taking an active approach to life by focusing on growth and achievement. You make a conscious decision to plant yourself in environments that promote personal and professional growth opportunities. You don't allow situations you can not control to dominate your attitude. You stay away from people, places and things that disconnect you from your support systems. When you are not Building and Developing, you are slowly rotting. Overtime you will wither on the inside with a minimized vision, stunted development, feelings of emptiness and a rotten perspective on life. The end result... stinky attitudes and behaviors. Building and Developing brings life. Rottenness brings disaster.

Whatcha gonna do about it?

What do you do daily to Build and Develop yourself and the people around you?

What "things" make you feel rotten about yourself?

What rotten feelings do you have about others? How can you seek to resolve them?

What can you do to address these rotten emotions this week?

- 49 -

"Work like you mean it, Play like you've earned it!"

Achievement is the result of hard work. It is produced by intense focus on completing the tasks at hand. Repeatedly handling your responsibilities results in success. Yet, those who achieve the most recognize that all work and no play leaves you broken. They also know that all play and no work leaves you broke. Learning to be creative and efficient at both work and play creates a well rounded and valuable asset. So, work hard, play hard, work smart, play smart!

Whatcha gonna do about it?

What things put you in a good mood? Write down as many as you can think of.

This week after you have completed a major project or completed an assignment celebrate by doing one of the ten things above.

Just like you schedule work, you must schedule time or yourself. This week write a schedule of things you will complete (date and time). Also schedule a time when you will do something for yourself to re-energize your mind, body and soul.

103

- 50 -

"Get the Full Experience!"

We demand the best experiences out of our entertainment. We don't want to be cheated. Yet in life, we don't demand the same. We often just skate by, without truly enjoying the experience. Apples know YOLO **(You Only Live Once)** If we don't move outside our comfort zones, we don't get the full experience. We miss the possibilities life has to offer. Don't cheat yourself. Demand the best of yourself. Get the full experience out of life. The good, the bad, and the ugly!

Whatcha gonna do about it?

Do you have a list of things you have yet to achieve? No? Create a list this week. Be sure to include small, medium and large items. (Examples...Met a celebrity, take my kids to Disneyland, Pay off my debts, retire, etc...

Can you do anything from the list this week? Something small?

This week do something new every day. Something you have never done before! Go to a new store, try a new food, talk to someone new...the possibilities are endless. This is growth!

- 51 -

"In the end, what you did out weighs what you said!"

We live in a time when everybody can say what is on their mind and share it with a billion people instantaneously. Words are powerful and insightful. Words can shape one's public image. They can shape the course of governments and businesses. Like a knife, words can be a useful tool or a deadly weapon. However, words without actions become hollow.

Words paint a picture. Your actions sell the story. Over time your actions, become your behaviors. Your behaviors over time become your character. Your character is the true portrait of your existence and your legacy. It is your actions which describe what kind of apple you are, an Apple known for its value, or a rotten apple no one wants. Build your Valuable Apple Legacy today!

"Whatcha gonna do about it?"

Have you considered how you will be remembered in the future? What are the accomplishments you desire to be known for? If you have considered the future, the time is now. Please start writing. Feel free to continually add items to your list.

What actions and behaviors will you display this week to create a Positive Apple legacy?

How Bad do you want It?

- 52 -

How bad do You want It?

Dreams don't just happen. You must have a desire. You must work to make them happen. "How bad do you want it? The question implies that there is a price to be paid for whatever you want out of life. It means, "What are we willing to give up, sacrifice, change, alter and transform?" It also means, "How willing are you to achieve, perform, accomplish,complete, attain and realize?" Whether it is a person, place, thing or idea, success comes with a price. Success is the achievement of a dream. The final question is... How bad do you want it?

Whatcha gonna do about it?

Are there things that you said you would do but haven't? Please write them down.

How does it make you feel not to do what you said?

What do you do to change that feeling? How bad do you want it?

What will you do this week to "make "it" happen?" What is your plan?

110

You did it!

Congratulations, you've finished the book! You have just achieved your goal to read this book from start to finish. This makes you an APPLE! You had the Belief, Action and Determination to finish this book. You have learned our 52 ways to Shine. You have discovered that you are valuable. You are now poised to leave a positive impact on others. Now it's time for you to continue the process of building and developing your opportunities to show your Value and Impact. The struggle makes victory sweet. Remember, Preparation leads to Success. Success is a choice.

So, whatcha gonna do about it?

About the Authors

While working at Community Colleges Cleveland, Ohio, Frank Kitchen and Rodger Campbell formed a friendship while assisting thousands of students and professionals on the road to personal and professional success. Challenged by the same students and professionals to share their message, Frank and Rodger left their college careers and to become professional speakers and leadership consultants. What began as a challenge, turned into an adventure that took them from college professionals to full-time speakers. Faster than they could have imagined, they went from writing notes on a napkin to performing in front of audiences large and small in the United States and Canada.

Frank and Rodger have over 40 years of combined experience advising individuals, professionals and organizations. Experience gained from note worthy careers in government, entertainment, business and education.

Frank and Rodger wouldn't be able to Shine without the support of their families. A Special thank you to Kelly, Elijah, Olivia, Melanie, Austin, Micheal, Gloria and Sonja.

This is just the start of an impactful relationship. Feel free to contact us directly by email.

Frank Kitchen
Frank Kitchen Enterprises
fresh@frankkitchen.com
www.frankkitchen.com

Rodger Campbell
Sigma C Enterpries
Rodger@badbadapples.com
www.badbadapples.com

Please let us know how we can assist you or your organization with an upcoming Orientation Program, Leadership Retreat, Conference, Convention or Fundraiser.